Let's Read About Insects

FIREFLIES

New Lenox
Public Library District
120 Veterans Parkway
New Lenox, Illinois 60451

by Susan Ashley

Reading consultant: Susan Nations, M.Ed., author/literacy coach/consultant

WEEKLY WR READER®
EARLY LEARNING LIBRARY

Please visit our web site at: **www.earlyliteracy.cc**
For a free color catalog describing **Weekly Reader**® Early Learning Library's
list of high-quality books, call 1-877-445-5824 (USA) or 1-800-387-3178 (Canada).
Weekly Reader® Early Learning Library's fax: (414) 336-0164.

Library of Congress Cataloging-in-Publication Data

Ashley, Susan.
    Fireflies / by Susan Ashley.
       p. cm. — (Let's read about insects)
    Summary: An introduction to the physical characteristics and behavior of fireflies.
    Includes bibliographical references and index.
    ISBN 0-8368-4053-4 (lib. bdg.)
    ISBN 0-8368-4060-7 (softcover)
    1. Fireflies—Juvenile literature. (1. Fireflies.) I. Title.
    QL596.L28A84   2004
    595.76'44—dc22   2003062185

This edition first published in 2004 by
Weekly Reader® Early Learning Library
330 West Olive Street, Suite 100
Milwaukee, WI 53212 USA

Copyright © 2004 by Weekly Reader® Early Learning Library

Editor: JoAnn Early Macken
Picture research: Diane Laska-Swanke
Art direction and page layout: Tammy Gruenewald

Picture credits: Cover, pp. 5, 11 © Robert & Linda Mitchell; title, p. 7 © Diane Laska-Swanke;
pp. 9, 15, 17, 19, 21 © J. E. Lloyd, Univ. of Florida; p. 13 © Bill Beatty/Visuals Unlimited

Printed in the United States of America

1 2 3 4 5 6 7 8 9 08 07 06 05 04

Note to Educators and Parents

Reading is such an exciting adventure for young children! They are beginning to integrate their oral language skills with written language. To encourage children along the path to early literacy, books must be colorful, engaging, and interesting; they should invite the young reader to explore both the print and the pictures.

Let's Read About Insects is a new series designed to help children read about insect characteristics, life cycles, and communities. In each book, young readers will learn interesting facts about the featured insects and how they live.

Each book is specially designed to support the young reader in the reading process. The familiar topics are appealing to young children and invite them to read — and reread — again and again. The full-color photographs and enhanced text further support the student during the reading process.

In addition to serving as wonderful picture books in schools, libraries, homes, and other places where children learn to love reading, these books are specifically intended to be read within an instructional guided reading group. This small group setting allows beginning readers to work with a fluent adult model as they make meaning from the text. After children develop fluency with the text and content, the book can be read independently. Children and adults alike will find these books supportive, engaging, and fun!

— Susan Nations, M.Ed., author, literacy coach, and consultant in literacy development

On summer nights, tiny lights flash on and off. Fireflies twinkle in the sky like stars. Their bodies glow in the dark as they fly. They zigzag through the air.

Fireflies are not flies.
They are beetles.
A beetle is an insect
with two stiff front
wings that cover
most of its body.

The front wings protect the firefly's body. They protect its two back wings. The firefly uses its back wings to fly.

The firefly has three main body parts. These parts are the head, the thorax, and the abdomen. The firefly's abdomen holds chemicals. Its light comes from the chemicals.

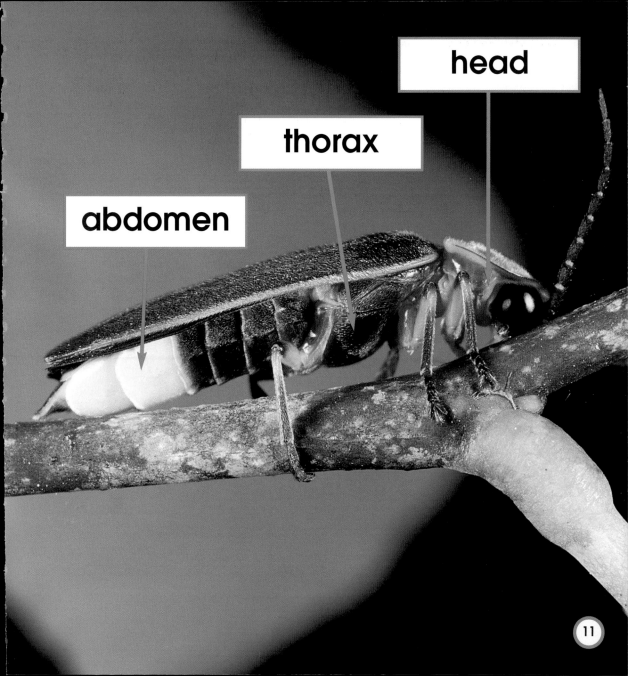

head

thorax

abdomen

Fireflies are often seen just after sunset. They are **nocturnal**, which means they are active at night. During the day, they hide.

A firefly glows to attract a mate. Males flash in the air. They flash in a pattern like a secret code. They send signals to females on the ground. Females flash back.

After mating, the females lay eggs in the ground. The eggs hatch. Wormlike **larvae** come out. The larvae eat as much as they can.

A larva turns into a **pupa**. It stops eating. It lies still. A hard white shell covers its body.

19

In the shell, the pupa grows wings. It takes on the form of a firefly. When it comes out, it is an adult. It finds a mate. The life cycle goes on.

Glossary

abdomen — the back part of an insect's body

nocturnal — active at night

shell — a hard outer covering

signals — sounds, movements, or things that carry messages

thorax — the middle part of an insect's body

For More Information

Books

Coughlan, Cheryl. *Fireflies*. Mankato, Minn.: Pebble Books, 2000.

St. Pierre, Stephanie. *Firefly*. Chicago: Heinemann Library, 2001.

Walker, Sally M. *Fireflies*. Minneapolis: Lerner Publications, 2001.

Web Sites

Environmental Information for Kids: Summer Night Lights
www.dnr.state.wi.us/org/caer/ce/eek/critter/insect/firefly.htm
Interesting facts about fireflies

Index

About the Author

Susan Ashley has written over eighteen books for children, including two picture books about dogs, *Puppy Love* and *When I'm Happy, I Smile*. She enjoys animals and writing about them. Susan lives in Wisconsin with her husband and two frisky felines.